CU00546161

IN THE SAME SERIES

1 – FIONA BENSON

2 – TOBY MARTINEZ DE LAS RIVAS

3 – HEATHER PHILLIPSON

4 – JACK UNDERWOOD

5 – JOE DUNTHORNE

6 – ANNIE KATCHINSKA

7 – SAM RIVIERE

8 – TOM WARNER

9 – RACHAEL ALLEN

10 – WILL BURNS

11 – ZAFFAR KUNIAL

12 – DECLAN RYAN

13 – ELAINE BECKETT

14 – CRISPIN BEST

15 – SAM BUCHAN-WATTS

16 – RACHEL CURZON

Crispin Best

FABER & FABER

First published in 2016
by Faber & Faber Ltd
Bloomsbury House
74–77 Great Russell Street
London WC1B 3DA

Typeset by Hamish Ironside
Printed in England by Abbeystar

ACKNOWLEDGEMENTS

With thanks to the people who made any of this possible
and for the publications in which some of the poems have appeared,
including *B O D Y*, *LEFT*, *Poems In Which*, *Roulade*,
Queen Mob's Tea House, the *Quietus*, *Hilda* and
I Love Roses When They're Past Their Best.

A CIP record for this book
is available from the British Library

ISBN 978–0–571–33040–9

'

2 4 6 8 10 9 7 5 3 1

Contents

poem in which i mention at the last moment an orrery 1

my god 3

they are building a building 5

fao: barack obama 8

the illuminati jokebook 10

poem at the dinner table 12

some mornings 13

anyway 14

allow me to change your life 15

i am a wildman in a white sweater at work for you 17

poem in which i mention at the last moment an orrery

there are certain
people i have only ever met in
the rain

i am a moon and you
are a moon
i mean i am the moon and yes
you are too
i am calmer when we're the
moon if you can believe such
a thing

consider the things my body is
for example there is a part of it
which is an ankle
another part which i can only describe as
the distance between distance
and distance
a part which makes a muffled
hopeful noise and another part which is
an ankle

on the moon there is an american flag
on us though there is nothing
just now

of the 47 nesting herons
displaced by the recent storms
47 died

i have stopped doing the thing you sometimes
complain about
which we notice at the same time
tapioca exists you've just
remembered and so tell me

oh my heavens we think and then
the word tapioca
together

moon and moon
tapioca

all the same there are certain people
i have never met

good morning pop music
is inside me like a wind
pop music is in me like
gas in the moon

there is an orrery
of us
i have seen it behind
glass and it is true

my god

you have no idea
of the distances i would travel
just to disappoint you

i will even wear a fashionable shoe
my god
just watch me

another? i ask
go ahead you say

and another?

no that's too many shoes

we shout
we throw bits of the forest at the forest
we walk

the so-called trees and the sky
a so-called kite and a cloud
my god
the so-called sky but first the trees

if you hold my hand
hold my hand
it could even rain

a walk in the wet leaves

my so-called shoe comes off in the mud

my god these yellow socks

i love them

they are building a building

is it still brunch if i am alone

in my dream
i found out that my dad
was a wheelie bin
and i hugged the wheelie bin
and my mum said
'not that wheelie bin'
but i stayed hugging it

i have been thinking
about the time the universe
was the size of a cantaloupe

oh my

there are things i have
been confused about

there are things about which
i have been confused

when i asked if things are serious
with your new boyfriend
did you say you are just dating
or gestating

i wish for you pancakes
bells
a wicker fence
a cat bewildered
bells in the distance

[5]

a cat in heat trying
to flirt with a wicker fence
i wish for you bells

i have crushed cans
while thinking of you

i have also cradled
a croissant
like a baby
so

i wish for you sirens going off like milk
i wish for you the evening
foxes sneezing in the streets below
the night

i wish for you butterflies in the airport

i have been thinking of the universe
it never gets older when i read how old it is
the sun paints me brightly
polishes the daymoon
above my head
oh my

i wish for you a warm balcony
far-off planes made big by sunset
to own at least one loveseat in your lifetime
the most beautiful waitress
i wish for you a bird screaming on a church roof
while you are trying to sleep

dusk is a good word to say during dusk

i wish for you
my heart is beating like a whisk

i wish for you birds
to find an uninflated balloon in your pocket
i wish for you the perfect banana
bluebirds for you
birds
a person waving down from the fifteenth floor excited
cows
birds

cows

i have been thinking about the universe
even distant fireworks
make me think of the people who lit them
i can't help it

the builders are building a building

i will be honest
the animal does not understand
that you are photographing him

i wish for you the ocean when you least
expect it

fast running is good
i wish i could do it

fao: barack obama

caring about a person
is like asking a bagel
how to live

barack obama what should i do
with my only life and
what if v neck stood for
very neck

at every turn
people find things quite unbelievable
every cat has a dad
take a moment now barack
to consider the implications

inviting a person to care about you is like
telling them 'take a seat'
and pointing at a month-old pretzel

there is a music to burying things
barack there is even something
unbearable about escalators
if you need there to be

i admit i often want to tell a sunrise 'whoa'
like it is drunk and trying to fight

barack i cannot wait to have
a son and tell him
'you're almost like a son to me'
and then powerwalk away

i laugh at the sheer
machinery of feelings barack
with all my doors expanded
in their frames

a custard pie in the face
of certain death

barack it might be enough just to find
a longer hair in my sink
once in a while

caring about a person is like
praying to a doughnut in the darkness

still though barack
still my only life

again and again the grass fills this useless space
between the ground and the air

and again

the illuminati jokebook

i want to get drunk and look
at a candle with you tonight
snowboarding horses
couldn't stop me

i'm an optimist
that's what i like about you

i read about a swimming pool
next to a crematorium
they use the heat from
cremations to warm the water
that's me and you
those two idiot buildings

we're going to forget
so damn much when we're dead
like do cats get turned on
when we stroke them
and if no
why not

i am a long night at the river with you

if i ever become a stupendous bazooka then
please
shoot me

the peanut butter and jam both
ran out in the same sandwich
so truly
romance is alive in the world today

well now look at us
all green kissing
in the light of the exit sign

finally

poem at the dinner table

here is the thing: the real reason i don't let people   get close to
is this faux denim shirt   i'm scared that   they will be able to

einstein said   his second best idea   was to boil an egg   in his s
as it cooked   frankly i get halfway   through a sente
and want to break a tennis racket

at the dinner table   i ask   for your thoughts on wind turb
'big fan'   you say   we try not to la
and through the window   look at the bad clouds   being bad
the good clouds   being clo

here is the thing: there are even tiny movements   of your fin
that i don't   completely understand   frankly i get half
through a poem   and it's nearly n
the same sunset   has been travelling   around the e
for millions of years

it is good to be talked to   and also   to hear people s

here is the thing: between the boiler's ticks   i hear you whis
that you had a hunch   about the shirt

from this great distance   i make my arms the perfect len

some mornings

sometimes it rains. it
is good to experience
a train window. you
have often laughed at
the places i have put
my mouth. it is good
to experience a
moonlit reservoir.

those dark trees. that
palaver of leaves.

time passes like a
kidney stone. some
mornings it is
beautiful just to hear a
sneeze. there are
people so good at
frisbee they don't
even call it that.

anyway

i am riding lifts on my 30th birthday

somewhere you are all of my direct messages and
a little drunk with you on a train would be nice
anyway they washed the floor of the museum
so my footprint is everywhere on my 30th birthday
and my shoe bottoms must be very beautiful

somewhere i am a kite when you slam me into the sand

still
anyway i am sweating in the museum lonely
somewhere i am sweating not touching butterflies in the enclosure too
place your various parts close by on my 30th birthday
feel free

anyway these unshrinkable distances
still
anyway your knees in the morning

somewhere i am sweating quietly learning how to pick up a butterfly
on my 30th birthday
after i nearly step on a butterfly in the enclosure too
there are chrysalises with us here
touch my chest in my imagination

anyway take off your belt with me on my 30th birthday

still
somewhere i am sweating watching the pattern of your bra
complicate the front of your blouse

allow me to change your life

welcome to the poem
i am cold by the window

there are things in the universe that are
just raccoons

remember the reflection in your bathroom when you are there
remember the wild compliments with which it keeps bewildering you
'you are so beautiful i would like to break wind gently on your legs'
your reflection says

there is a cold lustre
to the worlds of redheaded girls and kitchen appliances
remember that
remember the part of you that knows
the exact moment a dragonfly the shape of a dragonfly will reappear
from behind the pepperbush

what about a 10ft restraining order where 10ft
is the furthest away you're allowed to be

'darling you smell awesome like a grandma'
your reflection tells you
what about the world's smallest octopus
how did it get so small

at least life is hell
remember that

what about how it feels to steady a lover when the train lurches
and for example could you gladly climb a ladder to lie in a bed
could you marry a bumblebee if it loved you back
i could

remember science is always doing something we don't understand
to the sky
for example how is this sky the pink of faded orange socks
how is it exactly that dark et cetera

remember somewhere on this planet
there could be a car park full of happy dogs
we are so very bookended
by not anything
what about that
what about competitive pleasuring of everyone

'i'm so hard for you like maths'
(your reflection again)

go ahead and remember bottled water

bottled water

there

and what is the highest floor of a building
you can imagine a horse being on
now imagine a horse on the level above that

you're welcome

i am a wildman in a white sweater at work for you

i am nearer to a fax than i have ever been before

and just think
next time we are together
hundreds of people will be sleeping in submarines somewhere

why wouldn't they

so watch me minimise firefox sitting in a swivel chair for you
bent and straightened beside the water cooler
eating soup at my desk at my desk
my doleful finger in so much phone cord

i would even bother the folds of your shucked off undergarment
listen i would literally wear a white sweater in an office if i had to

if i smile when i say
'these doors are alarmed?
why what's happened?'
i'm sorry
i am most beautiful while printing out emails
and yes when i think of you i am hard at work

you are the reason i'm looking round at a brainstorm
thinking
what right now are the different ways i can hurt myself
good sir we are on the fifth floor with an unstopped window
yes ma'am the projector's plenty heavy at that height

six minutes wild texting in a toilet cubicle
you are the reason for watching bowls rotate in microwaves
brewing cups of tea by windowlight

your email says italic text is named for the tower of pisa
while i see words leaning into a cold wind

i'm recycling agendas for you

hello glass meeting room table i'm falling through you
what if i just started eating the plants
the strings that control these blinds might take my weight
at the neck

quiet
here look i am
fluorescing